Yellow Drops of
STARDUST

Yellow Drops of
STARDUST

A collection of poetry, thoughts and art

 Miriam Otto

An Ink Gladiators Press® Publication

Ink Gladiators Press®
Publishing and promoting warriors on life's battlefield

Ink Gladiators Press is an ePublishing company whose mission is to publish and promote writers, poets, lyricists, artists and photographers through our current worldwide market distribution of over 3 billion readership. It is not affiliated with any other organization and is an independent ePublishing house. For Earthians who want to publish with us, check out our ongoing publishing opportunities at Our Earthians Community Group, or write to us to learn more about our high-end professional Celestial Sky Services at the following email address: contact@inkgladiatorspress.com.

First Edition

Yellow Drops Of Stardust
ISBN: 978-81-949418-8-0

Ink Gladiators Press®
Bangalore, India
www.inkgladiatorspress.com

Credits:
Photography & Art: Miriam Otto
Cover and Book Design - Leonie Belle Hawk
Editor - Reena Doss

Filled with magic, this book is for you!

Imagine this book becoming your companion
over the next day, week
or maybe, even for a month.

Let it meet you on your travels
as a friend or soulmate with whom you feel
a strong and spontaneous connection.
You might need it
when you go through your day.

You decide.
Let yourself be surprised. Feel at home.

Part 1

Stars and Other Wishes

I weave a net of magic,
catching shooting stars and hope.

I find yellow drops in niches,
when I dare to look
at the parts of me that are
still missing.

Sometimes,
they fly into my space net,
greeting me with a short hello
like shooting stars and wishes dropping in.

I call them hope
and hear their whispers
at night-time—
my heart's melodies.

And now…
I gift them to you
as a long deep conversation
weaving magic that you long for.

Let me invite you into my spaceship,
have a seat and feel welcome.
My name is
Pilot of Light.

Please,
collect some yellow drops
from the burning sun,
touch the moon's surface
when we sleep.

Bring some grey
from its soil and dust,
when you return to my dreams.
I will add them to my color palette
when I wake up.

Life is not always bright,
I need some dark shades
to obliterate negative thoughts
circling around my head.

I will use them like a blanket of stars
to feel warm again,
sensing you near me.

#*You are my sunshine*

I strongly believe
we hold a whole universe within us.
Like little worlds and endless realms
with vivid landscapes and stories
just waiting to be told.

You hop from one island to another
while you are surrounded by
waves of emotions
with crystal clear water,
so salty that you lose yourself
in the depth of it,
when you fill your lungs
with the breeze of the ocean
and the tips of waves on your lips.

Maybe you will find yourself again
if you dip into the now.

#*Your Universe*

I don't know if you feel this longing?

When I sense it, I dive
right away into the cloud of stardust.
This place seems to be far away,
but I reach it in seconds,
because I hold it within me.

The void tingles on my skin,
creates sounds
and tickles.

It holds tiny particles like stars twirling
around me
and I get hypnotized by their circling movements,
spinning in the same way
again and again.

It starts with a humming vibration in my bones.
At first, I see nothing,
but a part of a shining brightness
which blinds me,
appearing white with no differentiation.

When I close my eyes,
my heartbeats synchronize to its tune.

Sometimes,
I even get a white-out,
because I am used to the vast
darkness surrounding everything.

It is a feeling from the earth, maybe,
when you are within the desert
and the dunes rise high
around you,
when there is not much left of the sky
and the light fades out softly,
when you don't see your footsteps anymore,
because they are gone with the wind,
just a second ago;
then everything fades into one
and it gets hard to orientate.
You lose the sense of
top and bottom,
from left to right.
There is only one color
and you.

When I allow myself to get lost,
I will find myself again
and the magic which this place holds
will fill me up immediately.

#*My favorite place*

I followed the red thread,

a cotton cord slid through my fingers.
I felt the rough material
leaving an imprint on my soft skin.
Am I too soft, too emotional?
Do I react to everything, too quickly?
Why do I usually have the feeling
that something is wrong with me?
Like a puppet played by masters,
I try to please everyone.

But this time it was different.
Maybe I had moved on?

It felt as if I was guided by a path of words
in the middle of the universe,
as if I knew this foreign language;
this floating alphabet of singular letters
had an effect on my heart
like tunes playing the beginning of a song.

"Can a magician fall under a spell?"
I always wondered.
My answer to this now is,
"Yes!"

But suddenly,
I was distracted by an emotion
coming from the left.
I followed this sense
and left the conversation
with myself behind me.
I followed it
and fell and fell and fell.

Emotions usually open
a gate to a new realm.
They do not follow the rules
of the world, you know.

So it happened that I was guided
by a white stream of waves
like a fast running brook
surrounded by darkness.
Opening a well that never runs dry,
knowing instinctively
that everyone owns one.
Then in the next second—
I was back—as if
nothing had ever happened.

#*Let the words sink in.*

Feeling alive,
she felt something she hadn't known before—
anger arising…
And though she disliked what arrived with it,
it awakened a new energy within her.
Maybe this green dragon
had brought change and self-love
when she most needed it.

Maybe this creature was from another world?
No one will ever know.
A dragon can be a wise friend.
In the end, it freed her.

She needed
fierceness to go through this,
even when she felt that
it threw her out of her comfort zone.

In some instances, in our lives,
we will shatter to pieces
and recollect our bits like a puzzle.
We will become even more whole
even when parts of us may still seem missing,
we will find ourselves in the lacunas
of our cracks and splits,
in the darkness of possibilities.

She saw all this and knew…

She needed POSSIBILITIES,
STARS SHINING on her way
glittering with MAGICAL DUST,
lightning up the PATH,
not yet seen by anybody,
not even KNOWN to her!

She had always been THE WANDERER,
needing the breath of the OCEAN,
the constant changing WIND of the MOUNTAINS,
the scent of cinnamon and cocoa,
whispering to her from far-off PLACES.

She just sets one step after the other,
knowing that she will find out.

Part 2
Growing Into our Size

Listen to me,
whisper to my dreams
when I am still half awake…

When I listen, wonders happen;
maybe this is what we call magic.

Life happens
when I step over the fine lines
of my comfort zone,
when I leave my safe space,
when I finally use my wings
that were clipped for far too long.

Yellow drops fill my aches and cracks
that become healed scars
where flowers can start to bloom,
weaving alchemy in new beginnings.

I feel magic returning,
creating sparkling waves.

I promised to be BOLD.
Tall.
Not hiding myself.

Like a cocoon,
ready to grow into
my new size,
I stretch myself.
I open my petals
like a morning flower,
ready to fit in.

#Be bold!

I remember,
the first time we spoke to each other,
you created a mixtape for me
in the conventional way with a real tape...
I remember as if it were yesterday.

The first time I hesitated to call you,
I recognized that I was nervous,
realizing that I cared about you,
more than a normal friend.

The first time you invited me home,
you checked if you were taller.
This was so sweet,
always loved your dark, deep eyes
which were curious to know more
about people and their stories.

The first time you planned our date
to make sure that we were alone,
followed by that first kiss.

It's been years by now
and we still have many first times.
You always say that I
constantly hold surprises for you.

I know I get you out of your comfort zone,
you tell me regularly.
You like and dislike this
at the very same time.

Then you tell me,
in your soft, warm tone,
letting me feel I am home,
that it never gets boring
with an adventurous woman.

It is important to know
that we have to cherish the moment.
There is often only ONE first time.
Still, we can create new moments
over and over again.
And yes, sometimes it is hard work
when we have to allow each other
to grow and become.

I feel that every moment
is unique and precious.
The sand of time ticks
and we collect every moment
like beautiful grains
we call life.

#You

What I learned from you
and what I want to remember.

You can heal fast in many ways—
we can all fall in life
but getting up is easier
at our lowest point.

We just have to take
that first step,
one after the other.

#Dear Dad

Sadness,
can feel like a warm summer rain,
refreshing.
If you let go of the old,
the unneeded.
That drop of emotion washes away
what you don't need anymore.

Maybe, it is just a simple longing,
appearing when you feel the gap
between your wish
and reality.

Sadness has many shades and layers
giving you hints about the direction,
that is calling you
like your true north.
What about trying to find a new stage
on your journey?

Just allow your emotions to appear.
Maybe you will be able to move on
more easily afterwards?

#*True North*

I PEELED OFF
ALL MY LAYERS
SHADE BY SHADE
IT WAS ABOUT TIME
THAT I DID THIS —
LOOKING AFTER
THE REAL ME.

tenamo

Follow BLISS

where no past and no future is needed
like a drop of honey melting on your lips.
Catch snowflakes with your tongue—
feel the cold touch
and the instant cure of the moment.

Sometimes, it is about the melody
of a warm coffee to wake you up
with the fragrance of your favorite spice,
cinnamon or cacao;
the tune of your favorite song,
which you hear
over and over again on repeat
and it is the only thing you want
to take with you on an isolated island,
letting you feel happy.

If you sync with its movements,
you will land in the now!
When the air creates space,
it is the right time to feel
your favorite color again.

#Bliss

I find beauty within moments,
seeing love painted in the sky
when I listen to the melody of the leaves,
whispering from far-off planets
that I visit in my dreams and wishes.

It feels like the wind is calling me,
maybe it is the right thing to do.
I am not sure about it yet
but still, I strongly feel
a longing in my heart.

#Now

Author's Note

Dear Readers,

Thanks for being here and for being you.

My mother, Margitta always takes the time to proofread my poems and I cannot thank her enough for her patience and love. In fact, it was because of her help that I was able to submit my manuscript in time to the editorial team at Ink Gladiators Press®.

It was while I was sitting in a café—enjoying my mother-daughter quality time, the atmosphere of the place and the artsy flair suspended in the air—that I was inspired to sketch a lilac forget-me-not (it is planted with love into this book).

Travelling with me from Paris to my hometown in Germany, that lilac flower stayed with me and guided my thoughts until I penned them down. I believe in the magic of life and dreams and this is why I've collected memories like these precious moments for you. I believe in wishes and words and that poems can heal and soothe your soul. I believe it is important that we spend time with places that inspire you like the sun rays in Marrakech (it is the first photograph) and with the ones we love. Sometimes it is just about a short call or a text message letting someone close to you know that you are thinking of him or her.

I give my dreams a voice hoping this magic stays with you as they jump from my heart to yours. Write me a message and I will send you a letter.

Lots of love,

Miriam Otto

@miriamo77
Instagram | Amazon | Goodreads
Voices Of Poets | Translations Of Hope | Solace Publication
Website: https://dreamtravelconnect.com
Email: miriam@urlaub-marken.de

Tell Us What You Think

Write to us at contact@inkgladiatorspress.com. We might add your comments or reviews on our website as well as feature your Instagram profile. We appreciate your love for reading.

Thank you!

We remain at your service,
Reena Doss | Founder
Ink Gladiators Press®
www.inkgladiatorspress.com

Manufactured by Amazon.ca
Bolton, ON